SOLVING REAL-WORLD PROBLEMS WITH ELECTRICAL ENGINEERING

LAURA LORIA

Britannica
Educational Publishing

IN ASSOCIATION WITH

ROSEN
EDUCATIONAL SERVICES

Published in 2016 by Britannica Educational Publishing (a trademark of Encyclopædia Britannica, Inc.) in association with The Rosen Publishing Group, Inc.
29 East 21st Street, New York, NY 10010

Distributed exclusively by Rosen Publishing.
To see additional Britannica Educational Publishing titles, go to rosenpublishing.com.

First Edition

Britannica Educational Publishing
J.E. Luebering: Director, Core Reference Group
Mary Rose McCudden: Editor, Britannica Student Encyclopedia

Rosen Publishing
Amelie von Zumbusch: Editor
Nelson Sá: Art Director
Nicole Russo: Designer
Cindy Reiman: Photography Manager
Carina Finn: Photo Researcher

Library of Congress Cataloging-in-Publication Data

Loria, Laura.
Solving real-world problems with electrical engineering / Laura Loria. — First Edition.
     pages cm. — (Let's find out! engineering)
Includes index.
ISBN 978-1-68048-259-1 (library bound) — ISBN 978-1-5081-0065-2 (pbk.) — ISBN 978-1-68048-317-8 (6-pack)
1. Electrical engineering—Juvenile literature. I. Title.
TK148.L59 2015
621.3—dc23

                                                                                    2015021313

Manufactured in the United States of America

CONTENTS

Problem Solvers 4

What Is Electricity? 6

Generating and Using Electricity 8

Famous Figures 12

Communication 14

Television 16

Appliances 18

Computers 20

Video Games 22

Robotics 24

Medicine 26

Engineering in Action 28

Glossary 30

For More Information 31

Index 32

PROBLEM SOLVERS

Think of the many ways you use technology every day. Do you ever wonder how things work? For example, if you check a book out of a library, it is probably scanned into a computer, which records the title of the book and the name of the person checking it out. How does the scanner communicate all of this information to the computer?

The people who design our technology and make sure that it works right are called engineers. Engineers use science and math to solve

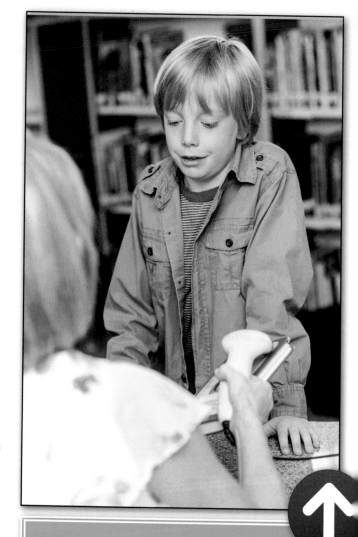

Library books have code stickers. The scanner relays the code's information to the computer.

Electrical engineers use tools, like soldering irons, to build circuit boards.

problems and to create new products.

Electrical engineers focus on electric power, as well as all of the systems and machines that run on it. They research, design, and create new devices, such as smartphones, air conditioners, and televisions. Working with other types of engineers, electrical engineers invent things that make our lives easier.

THINK ABOUT IT

Look around the room you are in. Which items do you think were created by electrical engineers?

WHAT IS ELECTRICITY?

Everything in the universe is made of tiny objects called atoms. Each atom has even tinier particles called protons and electrons. An electron has what is called a negative charge. A proton has a positive charge. Positive and negative charges try to pull each other together. However, two positive charges, or two negative charges, will push each other away. Electricity results when electrons are pushed and pulled from atom to atom.

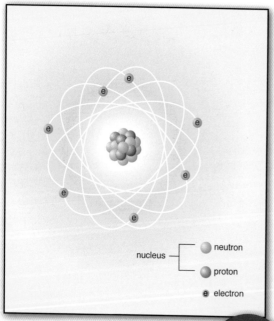

nucleus — neutron
proton
e electron

Electrons move around the center of an atom in oval-shaped patterns, called ellipses.

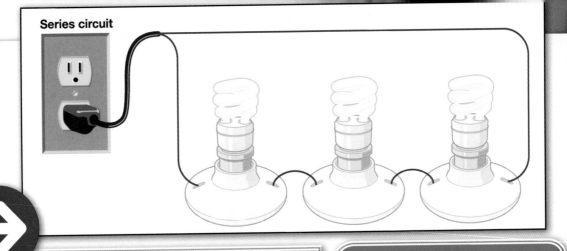
Series circuit

A circuit can pass energy through multiple devices, as long as the power source is large enough.

THINK ABOUT IT
Why might you want to turn a circuit on and off?

Many moving electrons are called an electric current. Electric circuits are paths for transmitting, or passing along, electric current. An electric circuit has to have a power source, wires for the electricity to flow through, and a device such as a lamp or a motor that uses the electric current. All of these parts must be connected for the current to continue to flow. A switch can connect the circuit in the "on" position and break it in the "off" position.

GENERATING AND USING ELECTRICITY

The electricity used for lighting, heating, and running appliances is made by machines called generators. Generators cause a current to flow by moving a magnet past a coil of wire. This pushes electrons through the coil's wires.

Many power plants generate electric power by burning

This system collects steam from the boiling water and reuses it to produce energy.

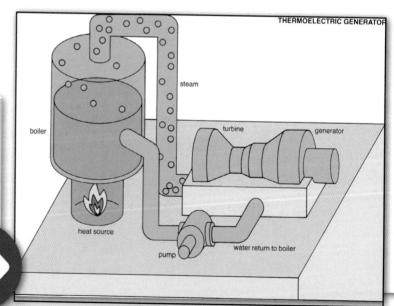

THERMOELECTRIC GENERATOR

steam

boiler

turbine

generator

heat source

pump

water return to boiler

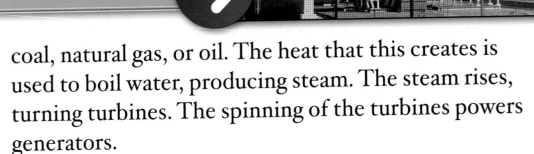

coal, natural gas, or oil. The heat that this creates is used to boil water, producing steam. The steam rises, turning turbines. The spinning of the turbines powers generators.

Hydroelectric plants use moving water—most often from rivers—to spin the turbines that power generators. Nuclear power plants use heat created by nuclear fission to produce steam that powers the turbines. Nuclear fission is the splitting of the nucleus, or center, of an atom.

A series of wires and transformers distributes electricity from power plants. The transformers change the voltage of the electricity

Voltage is the force of an electrical current that is measured in volts.

produced by the plant. This lets the electricity travel more easily over long distances.

A vast network of high-voltage power lines distributes electricity from power plants. It includes both overhead wires and underground cables. Transformers reduce the voltage so that homes, schools, and businesses can use the electricity.

Wires carry the current into buildings. More wires connect to the power outlets in rooms. When a person plugs in an iron or other electric device, the current travels into the device and makes it work.

Not everything that uses electricity draws power from wires. A chemical reaction in a battery can also produce an electric current. A battery contains two

Towers are linked together to deliver electricity to customers.

Batteries must be lined up so that the positive and negative ends touch in order to complete the circuit.

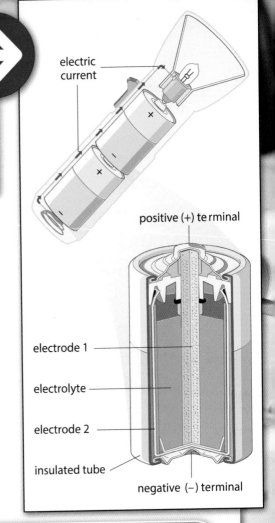

electric current

positive (+) terminal

electrode 1

electrolyte

electrode 2

insulated tube

negative (–) terminal

pieces of metal, called electrodes, in a mix of chemicals, called the electrolyte. Each electrode has a point, called a terminal, which sticks out of the battery. For a battery to work, an outside wire must link the terminals. Then chemicals in the electrolyte cause electrons to flow from one electrode to the other.

COMPARE AND CONTRAST

What are the advantages and disadvantages of electrical devices that use batteries compared to those that plug in?

FAMOUS FIGURES

There have been many inventors, or early electrical engineers, who discovered ways to use electricity. In the 1800s, Samuel Morse created an electrical communication system called the telegraph. It let people send messages over a wire using a code. An operator would press a key in different ways, opening and closing the circuit. It spread across America and eventually the world.

Another inventor, Thomas Edison, turned his knowledge gained as a young telegraph operator into new electrical inventions. He was responsible for the

Telegraph operators would tap the black circle on this device, called a straight key.

Nikola Tesla's ideas were challenged by other inventors of his time.

first electric lightbulb and the first electrical power system.

By the end of the century, a young man named Nikola Tesla had turned the world of electricity upside down when he discovered a way to make the flow of electricity change direction. Many people did not believe that his alternating current would work, but it is still used today.

Alternating means switching back and forth.

COMMUNICATION

For most of human history, communicating over long distances could take weeks or even months. Electrical engineers have come up with many ways to make communicating faster, easier, and cheaper. The electric telegraph could send messages, but they were short and only went one way at a time. Two-way communication was the next major development to come.

The first telephone was invented by Alexander Graham Bell

Alexander Graham Bell's first telephone call was to his assistant, who was in the same building.

COMPARE AND CONTRAST
Voice communication is faster, yet many people choose to send text messages. What are the advantages of each form of communication?

in 1876. It converted the human voice into electrical signals, which were sent over wires. When the phone on the other end picked up, the signal was converted back into sound. Today, phone signals can also be passed through fiber-optic cables and satellite signals. Smartphones, signaling over wireless Internet connections, are common today.

Smartphones have multiple functions. They can transmit sound, text, and images.

15

TELEVISION

The first television, or TV, combined technologies used in telephones and telegraphs with new electrical components, like the cathode ray tube. This component sent a hot stream of electrons through a glass tube, which hit the TV screen and created an image.

"Tube" televisions worked this way for many years, until the invention of plasma and LCD televisions. These newer devices do not use tubes, so they are much slimmer than older units.

The tubes used in older televisions required a large cabinet to hold them.

They send electricity through a liquid or a gas, which creates the light needed for a picture to be displayed.

At first, TV signals were sent over the air as radio waves that were caught by antennas on people's homes. Now, they are also sent through underground cables, for what we call cable TV. Signals can also be sent by satellite. Along with TVs, digital video recorders (DVRs) and other devices now receive the signals.

> **Signals** are the sounds and pictures sent to your TV.

> Television components have gotten much smaller and the screens much larger.

APPLIANCES

Most of the appliances in your kitchen are powered by electricity. For example, a refrigerator uses a compressor, powered by a small motor. The compressor moves cooling fluid through coils while pulling heat out. A toaster works by letting electricity flow through wires, which creates heat. The lever you press to put the toast down closes the circuit.

In a microwave oven, electricity passes through a magnetron tube to create microwaves. These are sent through the oven by a small fan. These waves of energy bounce around inside the oven, heating the food.

Toasters, coffeemakers, and other small appliances use electricity to make cooking easier and faster.

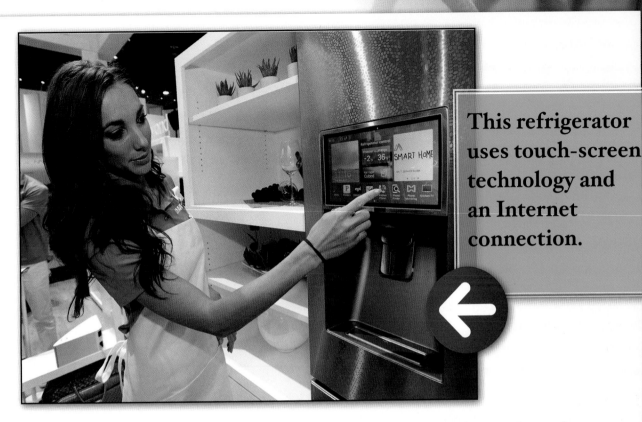

This refrigerator uses touch-screen technology and an Internet connection.

Some appliances use "smart" technology. People can use their smartphones to preheat their ovens. There are refrigerators that have touch screens built in to their doors and can sense when the door has accidentally been left open.

THINK ABOUT IT
How have electrical engineers made cooking food safer?

Computers

Computers are an important part of school and work today. They run on electricity and process data, or information, very quickly. The microprocessor, or brain of the computer, is made of transistors that control the flow of electricity. Transistors are like switches— they can only be on or off. The on and off positions are expressed as the numbers 0 and 1. Combinations of those two numbers make up a computer language called binary code.

Over the years, electrical and computer engineers have worked to make components

In schools, each student can use a separate computer to work on separate projects.

COMPARE AND CONTRAST

What are the advantages of tablets? What are the advantages of bigger computers?

smaller and more powerful. Computers were once large enough to take up whole rooms. Today's tablet computers are small enough to carry with one hand. Modern computers save a lot of space and weight by using integrated circuits, called chips, to store billions of tiny transistors. Storing data can be done virtually, using cloud technology. This means saving your work on the Internet.

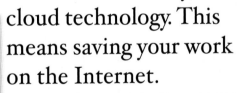

Large amounts of information can be stored in very small computer chips.

VIDEO GAMES

With the invention of computers came video games. All video game consoles are controlled by a computer, which receives the game from software or over the Internet. Players send and receive electronic signals to and from the game through controllers.

The earliest video games were played on a computer, using the keyboard as controls. Your parents may have also played video games at an arcade. These games were tall and boxy. Most had poor graphics. The entire game might be played on one screen. Your parents may also

The first video game systems were very simple but required bulky equipment.

have had an older game system, which had simple controllers connected by wires to a box.

Many newer game systems have advanced controllers, with motion sensors. The controller picks up how the player's hand is moving and converts the information into an electrical signal, which is sent to the game console. Another feature of modern gaming is online play, in which users can connect with friends over the Internet to play together.

Motion sensors are devices that sense movement.

Newer video games allow users to be more active and to play with more people.

ROBOTICS

A robot is a machine that does tasks without the help of a person. Many people think of robots as machines that look and act like people. Most robots, though, do not look like people. And robots do only what a person has built them to do.

Most robots are computer-controlled devices with many parts. Motors move the parts. Robots are used for dangerous or difficult tasks in manufacturing, medicine, and exploration.

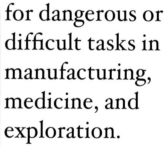

NASA's space rovers explore planets that people cannot travel to.

Students who are interested in robotics can join school clubs called robotics teams. They build the robots, give them commands, and compete against other clubs. At the competition, each team's robot must perform a series of tasks, called missions. A mission might be picking up an object and carrying it a certain distance. This sounds simple, but it requires months of planning to achieve. The robot that makes the fewest mistakes wins.

THINK ABOUT IT

When would it be best to use a robot instead of a person for a job?

Students of all ages can learn to program robots. Many robotics clubs use LEGO® kits.

MEDICINE

Doctors use electrical technology in a number of ways. The simplest way is computer record keeping. Handwritten records can be lost, destroyed, or hard to read. Computer records are more accurate and take up less space than paper files.

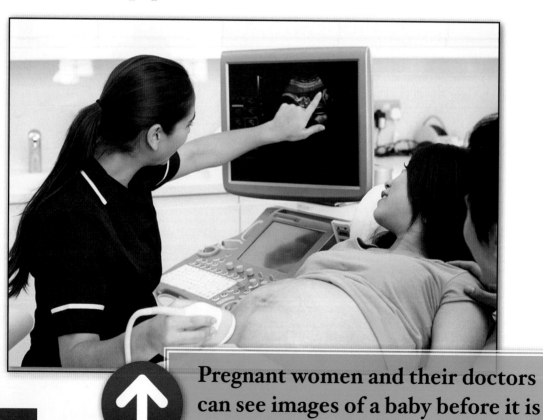

Pregnant women and their doctors can see images of a baby before it is born with an ultrasound machine.

To **diagnose** a patient is to find out what is making him or her ill.

Electrical engineers have worked with medical scientists to create machines that use electricity to diagnose diseases. Ultrasound machines apply electricity to crystals, which create sound waves that travel through the body. Images are taken from the bouncing of the sound waves, so doctors can see inside the body.

A defibrillator fits in the palm of your hand, but it is a complex device that saves lives.

Electrical devices can help weak organs work properly. A defibrillator is a device placed inside a heart that does not beat normally. When it senses the heart is beating too fast or too weakly, it sends a current out to get the heart back to a regular rhythm.

Engineering in Action

Materials:
- Small lightbulb (flashlight bulbs work well)
- C or D battery
- Two plastic-coated wires, ends stripped
- Tape

Procedure:
1. Tape one wire to the positive side of the battery.
2. Connect this wire to the bulb by wrapping it around the base. Be sure it is touching the metal part.
3. Wrap the second wire around the base of the bulb.
4. Tape the free end of the second wire to the negative side of the battery.

Did your bulb light up? Congratulations, you have just created an electrical circuit! To turn the light off, disconnect one end of one wire.

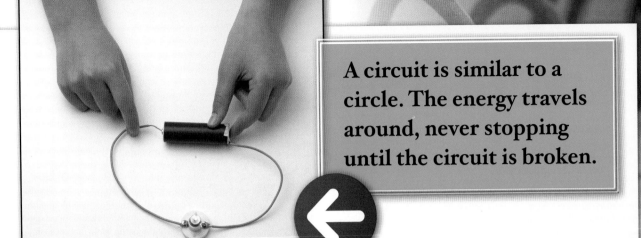

A circuit is similar to a circle. The energy travels around, never stopping until the circuit is broken.

If your bulb failed to light up:
- Check to make sure your wires are connected firmly.
- Use a little aluminum foil or a paper clip to make your connections stronger.
- Connect two batteries, end to end, with tape. Place foil between the batteries to boost the power.

The circuit you create is a basic version of what makes a string of lights work.

GLOSSARY

accurate Correct; free from mistakes.

battery A container that stores energy until it is needed.

chemical A substance that creates a reaction when combined with another substance.

circuit A complete path of electric currents.

components Parts of something.

compressor A machine that presses something together.

converted Changed from one substance, form, use, or unit to another.

current A stream of electric charge.

devices Pieces of equipment to serve a special purpose.

generators Machines that change other forms of energy into electricity.

integrated circuit Tiny group of electronic devices and their connections that is produced on a small slice of material (as silicon).

modern Of the present time.

operator A person who controls a machine.

power plant A building where electricity is produced.

process To take in and organize for understanding.

reaction A chemical transformation or change.

research To study a subject.

rhythm Steady beat.

software Programs or instructions that tell computer hardware what to do.

technology The use of science in solving problems (as in industry or engineering).

transformers Devices that change the level of power in electricity.

transistor An electronic device that is used to control the flow of electricity in electronic equipment.

FOR MORE INFORMATION

Books

Bow, James. *Electrical Engineering and the Science of Circuits*. New York, NY: Crabtree Publishing Company, 2013.

Ceceri, Kathy. *Robotics: Discover the Science and Technology of the Future with 20 Projects* (Build It Yourself). White River Junction, VT: Nomad Press, 2012.

Graham, Ian. *You Wouldn't Want to Live Without Electricity.* Chicago, IL: Children's Press, 2014.

Rusch, Elizabeth. *Electrical Wizard: How Nikola Tesla Lit Up the World.* Somerville, MA: Candlewick, 2013.

VanFleet, Carmella. *Explore Electricity! With 25 Great Projects.* White River Junction, VT: Nomad Press, 2013.

Websites

Because of the changing nature of Internet links, Rosen Publishing has developed an online list of websites related to the subject of this book. This site is updated regularly. Please use this link to access the list:

http://www.rosenlinks.com/LFO/Electric

INDEX

alternating current, 13
appliances, 8, 18–19
atoms, 6, 9

batteries, 10–11
Bell, Alexander Graham, 14–15

cloud technology, 21
compressor, 18
computer record keeping, 26
computers, 4, 20–21, 22, 26,

defibrillator, 27

Edison, Thomas, 12–13
electrical engineers, 5, 14, 20, 27
electric circuits, 7, 12, 18

electric current, 7, 8, 9, 10, 13, 27
electricity, 5, 6–7, 8–11, 12, 13, 17, 18, 20, 27
electrons, 6, 7, 8

generators, 8, 9

hydroelectric plants, 9

integrated circuits, 21

lightbulb, 13

medicine, 26–27
microprocessors, 20
microwave ovens, 18
Morse, Samuel, 12

nuclear power plants, 9

power plants, 8–9, 10
protons, 6

refrigerators, 18, 19
robotics, 24–25

smartphones, 5, 15, 19
"smart" technology, 19

telegraph, 12, 14, 16
telephone, 14–15, 16
televisions, 5, 16–17
Tesla, Nikola, 13
transformers, 9, 10
transistors, 20, 21

ultrasound machines, 27

video games, 22–23
voltage, 9–10